T0354861

DEFYING ENTROPY

DEFYING ENTROPY

A COLLECTION OF POEMS

DONNA HARLAN

DEFYING ENTROPY
A COLLECTION OF POEMS

iUniverse books may be ordered through booksellers or by contacting:

iUniverse
1663 Liberty Drive
Bloomington, IN 47403
www.iuniverse.com
844-349-9409

Interior Images Credit page 70 and 80: Becky Harlan

ISBN: 978-1-6632-6071-0 (sc)
ISBN: 978-1-6632-6072-7 (hc)
ISBN: 978-1-6632-6073-4 (e)

Library of Congress Control Number: 2024909551

Print information available on the last page.

iUniverse rev. date: 05/30/2024

CONTENTS

Linger

Cresting on Mount Ararat

In Conclusion

PREFACE

I remember my high school chemistry teacher talking to me in the lunch line, telling me I should have taken physics. If I had made that wise choice, I would have learned the second law of thermodynamics at a much younger age. As it was, I learned it years later from my husband, whose undergraduate degree was in chemical engineering.

For those of you like me who opted out of physics, one broad definition of *entropy* is a "gradual decline into disorder." Because this law manifests in our everyday lives, we must do many things to take care of ourselves and the world around us—recenter ourselves, dust, wash the porch, go to the dermatologist. We must learn to kiss the day with all its disorder and descent into disorder, even as we strive to maintain and improve our place in life.

This collection of poems reflects that constant reshaping and remaking of the world. Poems about memories are attempts to keep the mental cobwebs dusted from my brain so that those memories can remain alive. Poems about family tell of the redemption that love brings to relationships. In the natural world around us, we see and celebrate the seasons of life with death and rebirth, which of course also foreshadow events in the spiritual realm.

I find myself moving quickly between lightheartedness and more profound thought, but don't be deceived. Even in the most lighthearted poems, there is deeper thought, and even in the serious tones, there is joy to be found.

Yes, the natural world is constantly moving toward disorder, but there is a greater Power who brought order out of chaos as time began. He will do it again.

This book is dedicated to those whose very presence in my life
brings joy and peace, even amidst the chaos:
My husband Jim, daughters Katie and Becky,
sons-in-law Noah and Todd,
and grandchildren Lily, Maggie, Gus and Felix.
Thank you for being you.

KISS THE DAY

PLAYING WITH TRAINS

Someday I'll awake and want breakfast
before I want to play with trains,
unlike today,
which seems like every other day.

One day I'll awake and forget to play.

Isn't that the way of life,
always the same until it isn't,
and then you'll grieve the loss
of what you never thought you'd miss?

So, kiss the day with all its flaws,
its tears, and all its longings.
Hug me till my storm is past,
for with today, tomorrow is cast.

BURIED TREASURE

The Lego brick slides under the furniture,
making retrieval impossible without moving the bed.
I have no intention of going after it
not because I don't want to, but because
someday in the future, near or far,
I will have reason to move it,
and I will find the toy as a delightful memory
from a day spent with a nearly three-year-old.
I will recall that Lego bricks are soup ingredients
and train cargo and a feast of color that feeds imagination,
constructing a bridge that connects two people born six decades
apart.

I'll have to collect the other hundreds of bricks
strewn across the expanse of the floor,
secretly glad that I know about the hidden one,
a buried treasure marking a spot of joy remembered.

BE A BABY

Breathe.

You don't have to earn the right.

Cry if you need to, or want to, or if it makes you feel better.

Eat when you're hungry. With abandon.

Sleep when you're tired.

Watch things that move.

Watch things that don't move.

Make eye contact.

Reflect the emotions of those around you.

If you don't get what you need, keep trying.

Laugh because it feels good.

Let people hold you.

Let people rock your world.

Listen when people talk.

Move to music.

Trust people who know more.

Recognize love.

Grow.

Always grow.

YOUR NAME

How many times have I said your name
as a preface to my thoughts,
as a thought unto itself,
as a resolution to my discourse?

You are the heart of my novel,
the spirit of my screenplay.
You are foreshadowing, midpoint,
catalyst, and theme.

You are my call to adventure,
my road forward and back,
my journey and destination,
my comfort zone and challenge.

How many times have I said your name
as the end of my sentence and the beginning of the next?

BABY BOY

He could not be less aware of purpose,
ambition,
or whyfor,
yet his accomplishments are more powerful
than any Wall Street mogul with a mission;
his résumé includes
growing hundreds of billions of neurons
that outrival any brain surgeon;
his portfolio shows
perfectly formed whorls
more delicate than a delft painter could achieve
with the smallest of brushes;
his curriculum vitae lists
the production of vocal cords
unique in their design,
and yet he has no current choice.
How does his voice reverberate
before it's even heard,
so loud and welcome
in our world?
He has formed identity
before consciousness,
and he nearly takes our breath away
while we await his first.

THE REASON FOR LOVE

For you, I wish love,
not because,
not for reason.

The best reason for love is no reason at all.

Yes, you are beautiful.
Yes, you are smart.
You're funny, and sweet, and kind,

but love doesn't mind when you're not.

For you, I wish love,
unreasoned and pure,
grown in a vacuum devoid of "because …"

Because the best reason for love is no reason at all.

TANGLED WEB

Nothing ever doesn't ripple—
no stone skipped without effect,
no word spoken not passed forward.
Knowledge born gives birth to change.

Time machines could not undo
the tangled web of what and who,
chaos good and chaos bad
following what we knew and had.

Nothing's ever solitary,
games of cards included.
No Crusoe or Chuck Noland
leaves stillness in their wake.

Forgotten dreams connecting
neurons and synapses,
cluelessly, we answer,
unaware a thought was there.

Perhaps in moments clear
we see a glimpse of after
and toss our stones to waters
where ripples lead to laughter.

FIRST TO KNOW

We were all gathered in a hospital waiting room,
her husband, parents, siblings, and children.
We had been shooed out of her room by nurses who had
things to do—
things involving tubes, ice cubes, and palliative care.

A five-year journey led us to this place,
a journey of despair, prayer, and hope;
a journey of unwanted, well-meaning advice;
a journey of incredible help and compassion.

We talked quietly, waited, milled about.
I volunteered to check on things,
completely unaware of the task I had assigned to myself.
She was gone.

Gravity bore down on me, paralyzed me briefly.
Would I need an audible voice to convey this,
and if I did, how would my lungs produce the air?
I don't even remember. I must have silently shaken my head.

We had finally been given permission to sleep;
something we had craved now became impossible.
Empty, dark, silent hours ensued.
The only blessing we knew became those who knew

what to do, how to set things in motion
for more impossible, inevitable tasks
that would eventually make life possible again one day,
someday.

A BUCKET OF CHICKEN

Thoughtfulness came in a bucket of chicken.
It wasn't homemade, and it came without platitudes,
delivered with a hug and smile.

When Mom passed, a wall went up,
not because I didn't want compassion,
but because the emotional well can be too deep—
too deep to respond to words,
too deep to respond to a lack of words,
but honestly, not too deep to respond to basic needs.

I didn't need the two and a half hours of handshakes
or the well-pondered verses of scripture.
I needed to be fed.
I needed to sleep.
I needed space to think and feel.

My doctor offered something that would be calming.
Sounded a lot like closing off the well to me.
No, some REM to see her again would be better,
some solitude to cement the good times,
years gone by without any awareness of the need to seal them.

The bucket of chicken fed me well.

POSTHUMOUS LOVE

I didn't love her,
my own grandmother.
When she passed at seventy-eight,
my eleven-year-old self-imagined love
was simply an emotion larger than like
(and I also didn't like her).
I didn't like that she taught me obedience
with a willow switch,
although the pain was less than the fear of the pain.
I didn't like that she wouldn't let me eat raw cookie dough,
and wanted me to gather eggs from a henhouse. And
I'm sure she never once considered playing with me.

She never told me about nursing two children
who died before they were grown.
She never spoke of her husband's death,
which happened before my birth.
I never asked her what it was like to churn butter,
to wash clothes by hand,
to ride horses for transportation,
to feed farmhands with decapitated hens,
or to have lived through two world wars.

I didn't see her tears,
her fears, her tired soul—
only her solemn face,
her stoic nature,
which hid the grace
that she, doubtless, bestowed on me
and all of those she loved,
in the only way she knew how to love.
She buried herself before she died
so that she could make sure that we lived.
I love her now. And
I'm sure she knows.

DRAWING NAMES

She passed five days before Thanksgiving,
which of course none of us knew would happen,
only that most likely it would happen soon.

She was lying on the couch when she said,
"You know why my family chose not to draw names this year."
It was part statement and part question.

She went on.
"They're waiting to see if I die before Christmas."
What to say?

I don't know what I said.
I know it wouldn't have mattered.
She didn't say it for a response.

She said it to let me know that she knew.
I have never felt more trusted or loved.
She opened her soul and let me inside.

The highest form of trust,
to let someone come inside your mind,
to the very core of who you are.

She was right.
She knew. And they were right.
I still think they should have drawn names.

TRAINS OF THOUGHT

My thoughts don't ride on trains with tracks,
destination known,
crosstie supported,
at safe and efficient speeds,
but fly like kites
long tethered
or sea-borne sailboats blown,
wind trusted,
weather beaten
but *not* beaten down.

Genesis unknown, and if you need to know
where I stop next,
climb aboard,
although I promise not that we'll arrive
anywhere,
but we will share the same air.

WHITE NOISE

Your little body is making me strong
as I carry you around from room to room
and long to lay you down
but not really.

I feel the pull like lunar tides
and lift you up to the delight
of my tired arms
and neck,
and back
we go again,

repeating ritual after necessary ritual.
Nothing more comforting than the white noise of daily life.

SOUVENIRS

She calls them souvenirs,
the freckles my dermatologist examines—
lasting memories,
these benign windows into my past.

A simple grace she shares with every patient,
perhaps a silent prayer celebrating no bad news to share,
pretending to see sandcastles and boat rides,
high dives and convertible drives,

a needed window for this windowless room.

Her clairvoyance and wanderlust dismissing,
I truly see beyond my own adventures
to the speckled skin of grandmother Margaret.

Dr. Taylor doesn't know she made my day
with unexpected memories of Sundays with family.
No beach trip needed.

BREAD

She was determined to make bread in a coffee can,
which probably sounds insignificant,
especially to most people on most days,
but this wasn't either.

It was my mother,
and she was terminal.
I think she knew, but I didn't.
Hope dies slowly at twenty.

The recipe spoke to her from a magazine,
and she responded.
Somehow it inspired her,
energized her until it didn't,

which was quickly.
We watched (stared) more than was helpful,
hoping she could finish
and feel proud and accomplished.

The sweet scent filled the kitchen,
and she retreated to her usual spot, spent.
I understand the passion now more than ever
to do, simply to do.

It was never about the bread, really,
or the coffee can,
but about what could she do
one last time.

She made that day count
while she still had breath and a little fire left.

YOUR STRAIGHT-UP HAIR

Your straight-up hair
reminds me daily
of where you grew for months
before you knew
of light and air and smell and space
and skin on skin.

I couldn't see you when
your tousles mussed within
learned to staunchly stand,
now fighting against the wind,
bowing not to gravity's force,
rising like a sprout so fierce.

A glimpse of strength left unrevealed
on ultrasound.

HOME AGAIN

You can't go home again,
and neither can I, but we will try
in snippets of scenes the mind springs,
tosses at us to treasure or to bury.

The smell of winter woods and salty sea,
whirling air in open-windowed cars,
taste of freedom from responsibility,
coolness of shadows and heat of sun.

Rush of running on a perfect day,
yearbook's words of best friends and crushes
burned into our souls,
a branding we choose and wear inside

and always will.
Part of who we are.
Never shared or spoken,
but there.

No, we can't go home,
but home goes with us,
tucked into the pockets of our hearts,
the wallets of our wills,

like currency that never ends.

TEN

My skin fit better then, when I was ten,
and yes, I would go back again
to jumping rope
and counting jumps until I missed
and making pies of mud,
deciding who I was and would become,
with Mary Tyler Moore my choice.

Time, I would slay you
to fossilize that age and leave the jury hung,
unable to determine who I would become.
To my thinking I was already done.

But now,
there's you.

You're here
at ten,
two generations later,
so happy in your skin.

I gladly trade those days of bliss
so as never to have missed you.

THINGS I CRAVE

Laughter with its superpower
Productive days and long, hot showers
Scallops slightly browned and sweet
Birkenstocks upon my feet

Hearing tales of family members
Smelling cider as it simmers
Sunny days I spend with friends
A yard that other people tend

Finding bargains others miss
Crossing things off of my list
Watching sunsets on the ocean
Those who treasure my emotions

Attending church on Sunday morn
Hearing news of those reborn
Sipping tea in city squares
Playing games of who outstares

Breathing air as seasons change
Singing songs within my range
Lying down on smooth, fresh sheets
Knowing life has been complete

SEASONAL WINDS

MORNING SUN

Sunrise,
I would know you
even if
like a mischievous twin
you traded places with sunset
and no one knew.

I would know.
There is no fooling
a lover of the morn,
a lover of birdsongs
and newness of any kind.

You are the bringer of hope—
fresh,
crisp—
a day starched and pressed,
ready to be put on and worn
until, like linen,
completely beautiful with wrinkles,
your twin appears.

HAPPY GEESE

The geese are happy today,
swimming separately on the pond,
spread out in freedom from fear and foul weather.

They teach me beauty,
sometimes in solitude and sometimes in sticking together,
protecting, sounding alarm.

Instinctual love, I suppose, or something like it,
brilliant in my estimation—

knowing when to be one
and when to be many.

THIS

This. This. This smell of water after rain.
This cocktail of wind and sun.
This letting go of things undone,

and watching buried bulbs arise
from ground once frozen, now alive.
This. This. This panoramic open bar

of endless blue and hues unnamed,
unfound in catalogs and stores.
This. This. This chorus of larks proclaiming

the end of winter's dark: a song piercing
the clouds that muffle the sound of rebirth.
This. This. This day of weightlessness:

heavy with joy.

MOSS ON TREES

Moss on trees.
Need I say more?

A thesis completed,
a best-selling novel,
a masterpiece on canvas.

Study it well,
how it loves the shade,
so unafraid of the dark.

Nurtured by rain.

I want to learn from its refrain.

Never proud,
but bold enough to speak.

MARCH

As morning waxes,
I hear taxis
humming with the birds.

As sunlight lifts the evening's curtain
ever so intensely certain,
March is singing songs of hope.

I add the beat of snare drum feet
and tune out thoughts competing.

This bill of fare may not be rare,
but ever so divine,
the wine of spring.

I am invited, never slighted,
nor you,
nor others breathing.

Don't be deceived by dormancy.
Be ready for the party,
and if you're lucky, this will linger,
infused in what you wear—
the vestiges of earthen air.

ATMOSPHERIC PLEASURE

I watch the sky,
not for signs or storms,
not for objects identified or not, but
because it's wide. Because it wraps the world,
this blanket of air that breathes life into us.

I watch the sky, knowing
the sun will rise and set,
clouds will form and flee,
stars and planets will glow,
and I will know it again, happily.

I watch rainbows, half rainbows
and double rainbows,
the parts as beautiful as the whole,
as beautiful as their prism twins or even triplets,
each defining the day as better than it was.

I watch rain in drizzles and sheets,
vertically and sideways, freezing and making steam,
refreshing and flooding, cracking with thunder
and percussing in harmonious rhythm.

I watch lightning on the lake,
fog on the mountains, mist in the morning.
Decades of delight have danced before me,
old as the earth, but as new as birth.

I watch.

SCANDALOUS HOUR

Morning fog skates across the lake,
a dance floor shared with geese
in this scandalous hour
before dawn chases the party away,
knowing it will return tomorrow.
It never learns.

Celebrating something every day:
Did they gather because of the spin of this glorious sphere?
Was it to watch the bass beneath
or see sleepy trees yawn, bringing forth tiny leaves
as winter turns to spring?
Was it to delight in the bursting of yellow on the bank?

Partners scatter.
Fog leaves the rendezvous, vanishing like Cinderella.
Geese will search for her tomorrow,
but today, I must remember this scandalous hour.

ABANDONMENT

Caught in rain, I commit, but
still, I am confined,
without choice or voice.

I cower, crouch,
as if smaller means drier.

But then,

I abandon myself, and I am free.
I breathe in the smell of Adam's ale.

I shift, no longer obliging drops, but
welcoming with open hands,
asking for more, embracing the cleansing.

A river to my heart is forged;
the dam is broken.

I am abandoned.

A WAY FOR THE WIND

The trees are bent to the way of the wind,
the sway of the swells,
the force of the fronts,
like the feet of the heeled
wearing shoes that pinch,
reshaping the form forever.

And a day will come
when the tree will bow,
almost touching the ground
in the loudest applause
of the thunderous roar
as waves pound the sand of the shore.

And the tree will stand
as the crowd settles down
and clapping subsides in its rise,
and all will know of the wisdom it showed
when it bent to the weight of the day,
when it made a way for the wind.

NOVEMBER

November's last vestige hangs on the birch,

a single leaf
twitching in the mist,
curling its edges
like an old man in an overcoat
turning up his collar
and shrinking his neck.

It clings tightly,
then loosens and hangs by a thread,
finally falling down like the old man
tripping in slow motion on a cobblestone,
descending to dirt.

WINTER'S ART

Tree sculptures stand
planted in pots of snow
left over by sunlight's inappetence.

Branches in mid-orchestration direct
a symphony of chickadees,
attendees frozen in rapt silence.

Snaps of breaking limbs, well timed,
percuss as lightning strobes
and murals, ever-changing, blink on and off.

Ginkgoes stood before the Common Era,
strong through centuries of dormancy and change,
dropping blades of amber gold, reminding us that *old*

is a relative term.

WINTER MORNING

Did the red sky burn the trees to charcoal
and melt sugar on the fields this winter's day?
Because it looks that way.

Did the lazy clouds find friends to visit
mirroring them on the face of the water?
Or perhaps they could be their daughters.

Did the birds learn falsetto last night?
Did they hone and perfect their pitches
so that all of us would listen?

Did my lungs expand to fill my frame
with no space left within
save the air and my skin?

A THOUSAND WORDS

This view is worth a thousand words,
and yet
I want to find each word,
all thousand,
and spill
      them
      out
like shiny frost on morning grass.

Cold's smell swells like a sponge in my senses.

This vision, enough alone,
still pleads for definition,
begs to be captured in unworthy words.

MARRIAGE OF FAITH
AND SIGHT

The tulips woke me from the front yard,
the color of sun, a pleasant alarm.
Yesterday, they teased me with a hint,
so barely there I could have talked myself out of it,
but today, the verdant green has peeled away.

Why must I run to see, to witness what I know is there
when I have seen before and have no doubt?
I dare not try to answer for fear I might decide
that knowing is seeing, perhaps a kind of faith.

No, today, I attend the joyful marriage of faith and sight.

FLIGHT PATTERN

Observing a flight pattern—
the definition of watching paint dry.
Real-time nothing leading to big-time something.
Going somewhere.

Once you're far enough away from where you start,
you can change any details you want.
No one cares, except a spouse,
which doesn't last long.
Everyone smiles and rolls their eyes,
meaning "We don't care whether it was Tuesday or Wednesday,
or how much it cost."

The story is not in the day of the week
or the cost of the trip, or the chosen entrée.
The story is in what you are thinking about
while you stare at the flight screen.

While you watch paint dry,
your mind etches memories on your brain,
sometimes confusing days of the week,
but always getting the sunshine right,
always remembering impressionistic images
with twinges of delight.

No one asks, "Did we enjoy that day,
that meal, that adventure?"
No spouse will interrupt to say,
"You got the mood wrong on that."

Coordinates don't matter unless you crash.
Details aren't significant unless they change you,
unless they change your story.

LINGER

LINGER

Learn to linger on the bridges of the day—
the first moment of consciousness when you awake,
marmalade on your tongue and the taste of tea,
clean morning air as you step out the door.

Practice a pause as you say, "Hello."
There's a person in there you know.
What do you see in their gait and their eyes
that you might not have seen otherwise?

Memorize the moments that define your soul—
the size of your spirit when sharing a meal,
a walk that clears away mind's debris,
the prayer you tuck into your breathing.

Learn to linger on the bridges of the day.

The world is bigger that way.

FINDING ME

My family never stuttered or
stammered or
started and then
stopped
because complete sentences were formed in our heads
before they were said.
It was what we did.
How we talked.
How we lived,
and I thought everyone else did too,
even through high school.

But Susie.
Susie entered my dorm room
asking, without waiting for an answer.
Interrupting herself.
Using half sentences and half thoughts.
And she didn't care.
Didn't care what anyone thought.
My world exploded like fireworks inside that no one could see.

This beautiful, naked speech freed me.
This joy of unrestrained tongue released me.
This was who I always was and didn't know how to be.
She had no idea. Still doesn't. No one does.

I'm sharing it.
Now.
With you.

LABOR DAY POTATOES

Dirt in summer was joy,
from mud pies to haylofts.
Never a day without dirt,
but all in the name of play
until Labor Day.

We walked behind the tiller,
picking up potatoes and putting them on the flatbed.
It wasn't work, even on Labor Day.
It was the grandest play,
the best of two worlds
where time ceased
and caked dirt stained our creases orange,
sun baking the clay into our skin,
no thought that we would ever bathe again.

Summer's harvest piled high enough to topple,
held together by sweat and hope,
ready to be stored in the dark, dank cellar
and wait to be called out in turn for soups and stews.

It might as well have been a theme park,
that garden I never want to forget.
And thanks to the sting from the yellow jacket
hiding on the glass of lemonade,
that day is seared into my soul.

Grateful for the reminder to pay attention.

SQUATTERS IN THE SOUL

Words can't be buried like hatchets.
Hatchets won't rise like zombies in the night,
zombies with tracking devices, seeking
to bury the living alive.

Words can't be thrown like caution to the wind.
Caution tossed won't be regained, regardless of loss,
but words will cyclone round and round
until they find and take you down.

Words can't be recanted.
They refuse to be orphaned by their speaker,
by their target, by their eavesdroppers.
They remain, unwanted children,
squatters in the soul.

TIRED

When I'm tired, oh so tired,
even the good kind of tired that makes you sleep well,
I want to just hang, like wash on the line.

It's enough to feel the breeze
and the nearly silent whisper of wind in the trees.
It's enough to breathe,
which can take more effort than I want to expend.

It's enough to let thoughts come to me.
I grow tired of chasing them down,
of hunting them and capturing them.
Let them hunt me.

When I'm weary and wilted,
not in soul or spirit
but in my bones and marrow,
I want to curl up like a cat in the sun,
a babe in the womb,
warm and wanted,
not for what I do
but just because I am.

INSIDE

People are like houses.
You have to be invited inside,
past the pretty flowers and painted shutters,
beyond the front porch swing
to where dust bunnies run under beds and desks,
where sun-washed floors have lost their fresh face.

People like their own clutter,
their own imperfections and rug stains.
If you're invited inside,
try to hide your surprise.

The window box charm may not extend beyond the threshold.

WASHING THE PORCH

I always wondered if Granny had any fun,
but when I watched her wash the porch,
I knew there must be a trace of glee
hidden beneath that solemn face.

Three sides of playground
drenched in hot, sudsy water
swished and swirled under her broom,
sloshed and swashed to the yard.

Never wanted to be a grown-up.
Really. Never. Not so much even now,
but a keen temporary urge emerged
on that gray wooden platform.

Twofold hope shone in rainbow bubbles—
perhaps Granny wasn't as melancholy as I imagined.
Perhaps there would be something waiting for me
when I was old enough to wash the porch.

TOMATO

Red and round
ripe tomato sits
in windowsill
still waiting to be the flavor
I want most for lunch,

but when I lift it, without thought,
my eye is caught
by the gray fur growing
on the other side.

I cannot hide my disappointment
at its loss, but still, I toss it.

I have to say it brought me hope
and imagination's savor,
not completely wasted
although it wasn't tasted.

BULKHEAD

I spent more time staring at the bulkhead of the plane
than at the Sistine Chapel ceiling we traveled 5,000 miles to see.
It wasn't because I had to.

Somehow the four shades of gray
and the overlapping triangles completely drew me in.
No, it wasn't exactly artwork,
but somewhere along the way, I imagine it was said,
"Let's make that wall a little more interesting than the sides."

Somebody thought that mattered.
That small space of wall became:
sunlight over Egyptian pyramids stretching for miles to an endless
horizon;
an art lesson about cool neutrals and how to name them for paint
swatches;
an elementary school handout asking how many triangles could
be found;
a page in an origami book;

the best kind of blank slate—
        a springboard,
                a nudge,
                        an unfinished doodle.

I saw a dozen Bombardier Aerospace employees
sitting at a conference table pre-pandemic—
no major wars, no recession,
time and freedom to focus on nonessentials.

I heard someone say,
"Let's decorate the bulkhead with a pattern,"
and then for the next hour and fifteen minutes,
all twelve people got excited about contributing something extra
to my flight.
I felt honored. Truly. Not making that up.

Those people put themselves in my seat so that I could have a
trip to Egypt
or eighth grade, whichever I chose.

I didn't need a tour guide to help me understand.
I didn't need to know what year it was created.
I'm pretty sure it hasn't been seen around the world or in an art
history book,
but it was meaningful to me.

Thank you for that hour and fifteen minutes of genius.
It spoke to me.

BOUND

She is raising five children alone under one small roof,
no less bound than the feet of yesteryear's Chinese women.

Always in pain. Paralyzed. Frozen. Never free.

Bones crushed; spirit crushed.
Toes broken; heart broken,
repeatedly, no hope of normal. Ever.

Yet, a smaller version of possibility remains,
like the four-inch shoes on the Chinese women.

A hope that resides partially in us—
that perhaps we will put shoes on her children's feet.

VIRGINIA DARE

I read the biography of Virginia Dare three times in fifth grade,
hoping to solve a question three hundred seventy-nine years old
at that time.

Perhaps the author missed a clue.

A black hole opened up and swallowed me.
You've been there too.
It's dark and thrilling in that chasm of mystery.

Virginia was born and disappeared,
and yet …
she walked me through a door I'd missed.

She stayed with me for three trips through those worn blue cloth
covers
and told me to never stop asking.

SAFETY NET

I always had a safety net
and permission to fall from grace
and get back up, redeemed and forgiven,
not disregarding consequences,
the almost perfect teachers of life.

Today, I grieve your passing.
You never knew a net,
never held a social compass.
No one understood you, because
you never had the freedom to understand yourself.

I wanted more for you.
I watched, hoped, offered, prayed, and today
I speak this prayer for you and others:

Blessed are those who live without a net;
may they fall into the arms of love.

PERFORMANCE
OF THE DEAD

I dusted yesterday.

Today sunlight poured through the glass,
awakening beautiful, dancing specks,
suspended particles floating on a sea of glistening air,

a brilliant performance demanding captivation and applause.

Silent cheers for their resurrection from the cemetery shelf of
yesterday.
Gone their dull, ashen grave, their relegation to corners unseen.

Today they move in synchrony,
in harmony,
with majesty.

Thank you, fibers of towels and dust mites,
for finding the light.
Thank you, pollen, bacteria, and soil,
for bringing reward to my toil.

DETAILS

I throw details into the junk drawer in my brain,
thinking they'll be there if I need them later—
dates piled up on top of names and places
like rubber bands, nails, and tape.

Someone on the radio said,
"Put your spices in alphabetical order."
Quick, easy, helpful.
I believed it.
It was.
But.
Once they're removed,
they don't find their way home

again, like history searching for its decade
or even century.
I do care, really,
but apparently not enough to let details
take priority over more important things,
like the color of the label or how much is left

in the jar or the expiration date, so
I resort to rifling again through the drawer,
through the spices, through my recollections
and collections, knowing it's all there somewhere,
buried,
until it's found
and then not.

ORDERING

Yes, I would like the sun and breeze and dim sum.

Also, adventure with a side of comfort, and dim sum.

Could I add friends who make me laugh and cry,
family hugs with long, sweet sighs,
time to process good and bad,
gratitude for all I have,
faith to walk through light and dark,
events that on me leave a mark
of growth,

and dim sum?

LOVELY

Tea is the elixir we share today,
the magic brew to remove the fray.
Nibbling and sipping, the perfect way
to share the things we want to say.

So, just breathe in and just breathe out,
and all your worries leave without
another thought or care or fret,
and if you do, then I will bet

the tea will soothe you well,
and then your heart will swell
with gratitude for sugar and tea
and everything else that happens to be

lovely.

CRESTING ON MOUNT ARARAT

MOUNT ARARAT

There is a knowing deep within
that He who formed our skin
and bones still owns this tent we rent—

this temporary ark we ride,
this hide that hides the Spirit's breath,
that shallows out our endless depth of soul.

When cataracts of doubt torrential
sweep away our worldly hopes
and sink our promises assumed,

receding waters soon reveal
a better camp of purer rest—
an Ararat on which to crest.

Our thirsty veins again restored
are flooded now with joy.

IF ONLY

I see the light more clearly in the darkness.

Blackness sobers my soul,
like harsh wind.

Violence argues for life
more convincingly than peace.
Sadly so.

Wish I didn't need midnight
to long for daylight;
wish we didn't need pestilence
to yearn for unremarkable emotions.

If only contrast
was not the great revealer of blessing.

If only a better day
led to gratitude and remembrance,
not greed and expectation.

If only.

CANON

All of us are Pachelbels
reflecting songs we've learned.
Echoes bounce from canyon walls,
the opus of our lives.
Perhaps we hear a masterpiece
and sing it to our friends,
and they repeat the lovely tune,
and all are blessed within.

But if we learn an ugly score
with lots of notes amiss,
we need new compositions
to drown the sounds of loss,
new leaders and conductors
to bring creations fresh.

So, if you know a lovely song,
please sing it loud, and sing it strong.

GEORGEANDMARY

Kit is hardly anything without caboodle,
or this without that,
like a couple married for sixty-five years
whose names can't be said singly
without first slipping on the verbal banana peel of *and*.

No spaces between the words for years,
leading to a pair with only one name,
a name greater than the sum of the letters
that can no longer be teased apart,
and when one is finally gone,
the *and* remains open-ended
until it's not.

THE REVEAL PARTY

My maker wrapped me like a gift in tissue and sinew,
ensconced my soul in flesh,
hid my spirit in coursing rivers of blood.

Every moment of every day, my buried self looks out
on the world, striving to be free of all that binds
the invisible me captive inside.

Unable to leave the cell, the inner lures the outer,
pleads with beauty to poke holes in the hold,
petitions peace to blanket my heart like a pericardial sac.

There is unity at these junctures of body and soul,
a shadow of things to come, an incomplete joy,
an appetizer waiting on a meal.

Captivity will end. Pardon and release are waiting.
My maker will tear away the tissue and sinew
and give flight to the weightless me.

FUNERALS

I've been to many funerals. Many.
Large and small, inside and outside,
formal and informal, long and short—
each different except for the lingering spirit of the deceased.

I've attended funerals that lifted,
heard eulogies that lightened,
sung songs that transported,
been washed in heaven's light.

I've mourned at other services,
sensing sadness in unfinished business,
awareness of a life not well lived,
unspoken words hanging in the air for fear of disrespect.

Is it fair to speak freely of the departed—
no breath to defend themselves
or say, "Thank you!" to a compliment
or correct details of a worn-out story altered through the years?

I won't be there when it's my turn.

I won't be able to tell my side of the story.
So, I must live it now
so that nothing will be left hanging in the air,
no unspoken truths that would ruin the reverence of the day.

LEGACY

What if
my most inspiring thoughts
are never captured as words,
but caught and kept as hope in hearts?

What if
my desire for a legacy is fulfilled
with no acknowledgment of me
because it is written in the lives of those I leave behind?

What if
someone gains his voice because I listen,
finds his stride because I walk beside him,
trusts herself because I trust her?
Yes, I will live on as everyone does.

I will live as I did with breath,
a kindness shared, or a hope snared.
I will be remembered in an expression here and a laugh there,
and those looks and laughs will ripple through years until
my name disappears,
completely forgotten,
forever,

my legacy complete.

TREASURES

We think our treasures tether us,
our goods grounding us like gravity.

We presume our belongings add breadth to our breath,
our holdings heartening our beings.

We learn late our house will not hold us here;
people cannot prolong our position.

No power in weight when our souls are weightless.

Life lies not in linen, but in learning
to love, to let go and cling to invisible cache.

We are born to fly away,
to be free from skin and skein,
to be released from bodies and bangles.

STRAWBERRY CAKE

Not sure how I got the flavor of strawberry cake into a dream,
especially long enough to wake with the taste.

No particular reason for processing my attendance at a baby shower
for someone I've never met, in a church I've never seen.

No idea who the people were, but I felt at home and aware.

What I do know—
the warmth and joy in that celebration,
housed where imperfect people gather and worship,
where countless opportunities to give grace have been missed,
where sins could be stacked higher than hymnals.

This church was applauding old life and new life,
proclaiming good news
to a world hungry for more than cake.

COMMUNION

Eyes, fixed on crimson and crust.
Silence, full of collective agreement.
Air, laden with regret and gratitude,
though tainted by thoughts astray. We are

bound by belief and blood,
related by rendering of bread.

Holiness, like incense, rises.

Different needs merge into one—
redemption—
as we pray for meaning in these morsels.

STAINED-GLASS WINDOWS

Enter these walls with me
and you will see that, faith aside,
there resides a presence of sacredness,
an aroma of forgiveness,
an awareness of the plight of man.

Even with your back to the light,
it's there, streaming through the colors,
the stains that outline stories of the past,
stories that will never die, kept alive
by more than a book or a window

or even these walls.

WHAT IS A PRAYER?

A prayer is something you wear in your heart,
words you store in your soul,
thoughts you carry in the backwoods of your brain.

A prayer is a refrain that sings you a song
like background music all day long,
never lost amid the noise.

A prayer is a carrier of hope and goodwill
tucked into your breathing,
connecting you to heaven.

WORLD AT WAR

When peace reigned,
we had nothing to do but feed the poor
and help them ease into a finer way of life;

nothing to do but raise our young,
create beauty, nurture growth,
and protect our planet.

We sat on our hands and waited
for problems big and profound,
for war and disease

because we didn't see
that sitting on our hands

caused these.

SILENT NIGHT

Sometimes there is a sacred sound in silence,
a sound I hunger for—
when the newborn sleeps,
his breathing barely perceptible;
when dawn breaks before traffic begins;
when families sit together as if mute;
when believers partake of the bread and cup.

Sometimes there is a sacred silence that bears knowledge
of the unexplainable,
a silence so profound
it drowns out the noise of busyness
and restores wholeness,
recreates consciousness,
satisfies undefined yearning.

A sacred silence came *that* night,
a void so great
that earth heard the beating of God's heart,
heard the star cast light on the miracle,
heard joy bubble up as tears.

Silent night.
Holy night.
Be still.
The Great I Am is speaking.

UPON A TIME

Upon a time, there was a girl
and she jumped rope,
concocted cakes of mud in sun,
and dreamed of what she would become.

She came of age against her will,
wishing life was just cartwheels,
but innocence and play
were powerless to change her day.

But life was good and rich and sweet
as love and children filled her days,
and as she breathed and slept,
her children left her nest

to make their own,
their lives, their homes.
Their children, too, grew unexpectedly,
as if she'd never thought that through.

Reflect, she did, on all her time,
the hours filled with laughter's wine.
Regrets she tossed into the wind,
and dared them to return again.

And she died happily, after.

THE TABLE

A reflection of Psalm 23:5

My first memories are stashed in every cell (except my neocortex),
locked, but leaking, seeping, showing up in attitudes and words,
in patterns of thought and responses to light and dark,
speaking out and staying silent.

Anyone who would remember them is gone—
anyone who bathed me or brushed my hair gently
or harshly, anyone who fed me or played with me
or ignored me, anyone who was angry or kind or neglectful.

All gone, no retrieval possible,
no security cameras or witnesses, but
my cells tell me that I was loved.
They tell me to love others.

All around I see unknowable memories
of those whose hearts are full of debris,
whose souls are flooded with dirty waters,
whose minds are cramping in pain.

There is no restraining order that will block
our skin from remembering violence,
no holding cell to protect our cells,
no expunging the past from memories never known.

Our enemies are free to taunt and hate and anger,
but ahead there lies a table in the presence of these enemies,
enemies of our past that we can proclaim powerless today.

Join me at the table.

IN CONCLUSION

NOT EVERYTHING HAS
TO BE A POEM

Not everything has to be a poem,
but isn't it nicer when it is,
when words rephrase themselves and take on life of their own,
like yellow grass in winter pleading to be called an ochre field;
like dead, motionless leaves resurrected to dance the waltz of wind?
Sunshine declares herself a spotlight on both good and evil
and maker of shadows timid and proud.
In first grade we learned how shadows appear.
Mrs. Sharp called it science, but I knew it was poetry.
Mrs. Mullins taught her students the magic of borrowing to subtract.
She called it math, but I knew it was poetry.
The Amazon rainforest came alive in my fifth-grade room,
complete with backdrops and a script,
something for everyone to do to make geography fun.
Miss Hebb called it social studies, but it was poetry,
plain and simple.
Another day has faded; another poem has been written.
I will read it in my head and wait for daybreak to usher in new verse.

PREVIOUSLY PUBLISHED POEMS

"Baby Boy"
Published in *Nine Cloud Journal*, 2020

"Tangled Web"
Published in *The Ripple Effect* (Poets' Choice), 2022

"Posthumous Love"
Published in *Departed Souls* (Poets' Choice), 2022

"Bread"
Published in *Wingless Dreamer*, 2022

"Marriage of Faith and Sight"
Published in *Words of the Lamb Magazine*, 2024

"Finding Me"
Published in *looking in looking out* (Willowdown Books), 2023

"Washing the Porch"
Published in *Tennessee Voices*, 2023

"Bulkhead"
Published in *Wingless Dreamer*, 2023

"If Only"
Published in *Finding the Birds*, 2020

"The Table"
Published in *Pensive: A Global Journal of Spirituality & the Arts*, 2023

"Not Everything Has to Be a Poem"
Published in *Wingless Dreamer*, 2022

OTHER BOOKS BY DONNA HARLAN

Clothing Memoirs of a Wannabe Cowgirl
Remembrances of Growing Up in the 1960s and '70s
iUniverse, 2008

Bench by the Pond
A Poetry Gallery
iUniverse, 2019

Printed in the United States
by Baker & Taylor Publisher Services